EMPOWERING WOMEN ABOVE 50:

Navigating the Journey to Serenity In The Face Of Stress and Anxiety

s

Claire Higgins

TABLE OF CONTENT

Introduction

Life after the age of 50 is an important chapter, full with knowledge, experience, and fresh independence. However, it also has its own set of obstacles, and for many women, controlling anxiety and stress becomes an important part of this journey. This book is intended to assist women with practical answers and support as they navigate the specific challenges associated with this time of their lives.

In this introduction, we will quickly discuss why women over the age of 50 may suffer increased anxiety, taking into account cultural, family, and physiological variables. Recognizing the significance of treating mental well-being throughout this stage, the handbook seeks to provide women with effective tools and insights to promote calm, resilience, and general emotional health.

As we progress through the chapters, each part will provide practical skills, lifestyle changes, and emotional support to help women understand, manage, and overcome the issues associated with anxiety and stress. It is our goal that this book will be a helpful companion on the path to emotional well-being, enabling a meaningful and vigorous life after 50.

1. UNDERSTANDING ANXIETY AND STRESS IN WOMEN OVER 50.

Entering the fifth decade and beyond gives a richness of experience and a sense of achievement. However, this phase might provide particular issues, including as worry and stress for women. This chapter tries to shed light on the elements that contribute to these emotional challenges, offering a nuanced viewpoint to promote understanding and empathy.

1. Social Expectations and Pressures

Women over 50 frequently struggle with cultural expectations regarding looks, job accomplishments, and family obligations. This part explores the influence of cultural expectations, highlighting the need of redefining success and embracing personal fulfillment at this time of life.

2. Life Transitions and Changing Roles.

The changing dynamics of family structures, such as an empty nest or caring obligations, can cause stress. This section delves into the emotional complexities of life transitions, guiding women through shifting roles with perseverance and a positive perspective.

3. Hormonal Changes and Emotional Well-Being

Hormonal changes during menopause and post menopause can have a major impact on mental health. This section provides light on the relationship between hormonal shifts and emotional well-being, including tips for regulating these swings for a more stable mental state.

Understanding anxiety and stress in women over 50 is the first step towards developing appropriate coping strategies. By delving into these elements, we establish the framework for practical answers and methods in the next chapters, with the goal of empowering women to confront this time with courage and grace.

Recognize Unique Challenges.

Life for women over 50 unfolds as a tapestry of various experiences, but it is not without its own set of obstacles. Recognizing and recognizing these issues is critical in dealing with the intricacies of anxiety and stress during this time.

1. Body Image & Aging

Because social standards generally exalt youth, women over 50 may struggle with changing body images. This part investigates the influence of social beauty expectations and develops ways for cultivating a good self-image, including self-acceptance and confidence.

2. Caretaking Responsibilities

Many women find themselves caring for aging parents or supporting adult children. This obligation may be emotionally draining. Here, we explore the emotional terrain of caring and give advice on how to balance compassion for others with self-care.

3. Career transitions and identity shifts

Navigating professional transitions or retirement can cause feelings of loss and identity reevaluation. This section investigates the emotional aspects of such changes, offering techniques for redefining purpose and rediscovering personal fulfillment beyond typical work positions.

4. Social Expectations & Loneliness

While some women embrace their newfound independence, others may struggle with cultural expectations or feel alone. This part tackles the whole range of social dynamics, assisting women in navigating relationships, setting boundaries, and making meaningful connections that benefit their well-being.

Recognizing these specific obstacles is the first step toward promoting resilience and well-being. Understanding the complexities of these challenges allows women to go on a journey of self-discovery and empowerment in conquering anxiety and stress.

Identifying Signs and Symptoms

Recognizing the signs and symptoms of anxiety and stress is critical for timely intervention and management. This section seeks to provide women over 50 with the knowledge they need to recognize subtle symptoms and seek help when necessary.

1. Physical manifestations.

• Persistent Fatigue: Feeling fatigued even after enough rest.

• Disruptions to sleep habits, including difficulties sleeping or staying asleep.

• Muscular Tension: Unexplained muscular pain or tension, especially in the neck and shoulders.

2. Emotional Indicators

• Increased Irritability: Feeling irritated or angry without a clear reason.

• Persistent Worry: Focusing on unpleasant thoughts and anticipating unfavorable events.

• Mood swings refer to rapid and severe mood shifts.

3. Cognitive signs

• Difficulty concentrating and making judgments.

• Memory issues, such as forgetfulness or trouble recalling specific information.

• Negative thought patterns include self-critical or pessimistic thinking.

4. Behavior Changes

• Social withdrawal is withdrawing from social activities and isolating oneself.

• Significant changes in eating behavior, such as overeating or loss of appetite.

5. Physical Health Impact

• Frequent aches and pains: Physical discomfort without a clear cause.

• Chronic stress weaken the immune system, and its makes individuals more susceptible to infections.

• Common digestive issues include upset stomach, indigestion, and changes in bowel patterns.

Empowering women to recognize these symptoms allows them to take proactive efforts to manage their mental health. If any of these symptoms continue, getting help from healthcare experts, friends, or family is an important next step toward well-being.

2. LIFESTYLE CHANGES FOR WELL-BEING

Prioritizing healthy habits

Maintaining total well-being entails developing good behaviors that promote physical, mental, and emotional health. This chapter aims to inspire women over 50 to emphasize practices that promote resilience and reduce the impact of anxiety and stress.

1. Nutrition for Mental Wellness.

• A balanced diet includes fruits, vegetables, complete grains, and lean protein.

• Hydration: Drinking enough water might improve mood and cognitive performance.

• Mindful eating involves appreciating tastes and recognizing hunger cues.

2. Establish a regular exercise routine.

• Cardiovascular Exercises: Walking, swimming, or cycling can improve mood and reduce stress.

• Strength training enhances physical health and confidence.

• Yoga and stretching can help relax and relieve muscular tension.

3. Quality Sleep Practices

• Establish a consistent sleep schedule, it will help regulate the body's internal clock.

• Creating a relaxing environment in the bedroom, with dim lighting and soft bedding.

• Limiting stimulants: Avoiding caffeine and electronic gadgets before bedtime might improve sleep quality.

4. Stress Reduction Techniques

• Mindfulness Meditation: Practice mindfulness to stay present and manage stress.

• Deep breathing exercises use regulated breathing to promote relaxation.

• Progressive Muscle Relaxation involves systematically tensing and then releasing various muscle groups to reduce stress.

5. Social relationships and leisure activities

• Focusing on meaningful ties with friends and family.

• Hobbies provide a sense of satisfaction and delight.

• Taking breaks to rest and unwind from everyday commitments.

6. Regular Health Check-Ups

• Prioritize regular health check-ups and tests to spot any health concerns early on.

• Open communication with healthcare providers to address physical and mental health problems.

Empowering women to emphasize these healthy practices not only improves their overall well-being, but also provides a solid basis for effectively managing anxiety and stress. Women who adopt these techniques can develop a robust attitude and manage life's problems more easily.

Incorporating Regular Exercise

Regular exercise is a terrific way to improve your general health and well-being. Here are some pointers to help you develop and sustain a consistent fitness routine:

1. Setting Realistic Goals: • Start with attainable goals. Aim for 30 minutes of moderate-intensity exercise most days of the week.

• Divide bigger tasks into smaller, doable milestones.

2. Choose activities you enjoy.

• Find workouts or physical activities you enjoy. Walking, cycling, dancing, or participating in an activity that you like enhances your chances of continuing with it.

3. Create a Schedule: • Plan your exercises ahead of time and regard them as essential appointments. Establish a consistent fitness plan that works with your daily schedule.

4. Mix It Up: • Incorporate variation to prevent boredom during workouts. This might include aerobic, weight training, flexibility, and balancing activities.

5. Begin SloSwly: • If you're new to exercise or returning after a break, start with low-intensity exercises and gradually increase intensity and time. This helps you avoid injuries and allows your body to adjust.

6. Add Strength Training: • Incorporate resistance or strength training into your program. This promotes muscular growth, increases metabolism, and improves overall body composition.

7. Listen to Your Body: • Observe how your body reacts to activity. If you're experiencing discomfort that goes beyond regular muscular soreness, consider changing your routine and, if necessary, consulting with a healthcare expert.

8. Find a Workout Buddy: • Working out with a buddy or joining a fitness group may enhance the experience and boost motivation.

9. Set Reminders: • Use alarms or calendar reminders to encourage exercise. A visual or audible trigger might help you develop the habit.

10. Prioritize Recovery: • Give your body time to heal in between exercises. This involves getting adequate sleep, being hydrated, and building rest days into your schedule.

11. Appreciate Progress: • Recognize and appreciate your accomplishments along the road. Recognizing your accomplishments, whether it's completing a fitness milestone or being consistent with your program, may be motivational.

12. Make Exercise a Lifestyle: • Transform exercise from a chore to a part of your daily routine. Consider walking or bicycling instead of driving, using the stairs, or adding activity into your everyday routine.

Remember, consistency is essential when it comes to exercising. Starting with tiny, manageable modifications and progressively increasing them can help you form a long-term habit. Always contact with a healthcare expert before starting a new workout regimen, especially if you have any pre-existing health issues.

Ensuring Adequate Sleep

Quality sleep is essential for both physical and mental health, especially for women over the age of 50. This section focuses on ways for getting enough restorative sleep while also building resistance to anxiety and stress.

1. Setting a Consistent Sleep Schedule

• Establish a routine by going to bed and getting up at the same time every day, including on weekends.

• Set a relaxing pre-sleep routine, such as reading or stretching, before bedtime.

2. Optimizing the Sleep Environment.

• Invest in a comfortable mattress and pillows that promote proper posture.

• Creating a calm and dark sleep environment promotes relaxation.

• Maintaining a pleasant, comfortable temperature in the bedroom.

3. Limiting Stimulants and Electronics before Bedtime

• Caffeine Moderation: Avoid caffeine usage before bedtime.

• Minimize screen time at least an hour before bedtime to avoid disrupting circadian cycles due to blue light from electronic gadgets.

4. Mindful Practices for Sleep

• Use relaxation techniques, such as deep breathing or progressive muscle relaxation, to ease into sleep.

• Mindfulness meditation helps calm the mind and lessen racing thoughts.

5. Addressing Sleep Disorders.

• Consult a healthcare physician if you are experiencing recurrent sleep troubles.

• Treating Sleep Apnea: Medical intervention can help manage this disorder.

6. Balancing Daytime Activities.

• Regular physical exercise throughout the day helps promote better sleep at night.

• Eat lighter meals in the evening to avoid discomfort during sleep.

Prioritizing proper sleep is an effective way to manage stress and anxiety. By implementing these sleep-enhancing habits, women may lay the groundwork for better mental and emotional well-being, allowing them to confront life's difficulties with greater resilience and clarity.

3. MINDFUL RELAXATION AND TECHNIQUES

Accepting Mindfulness Meditation

Mindfulness meditation is a powerful technique that may help manage anxiety and stress. In this part, we look at the concepts of mindfulness and offer practical strategies for women over 50 to incorporate this powerful approach into their everyday life.

1. Understanding Mindfulness.

• Present Moment Awareness: Focusing on the present moment without judgment.

• Acceptance is embracing ideas and feelings without trying to modify or fight them.

2. Begin a Mindful Meditation Practice

• Introducing beginner-friendly mindfulness activities like focused breathing and body scan meditations.

• Establishing a consistent meditation program, beginning with short sessions and progressively increasing time.

3. Integrating Mindfulness into Daily Activities

• Practice mindful eating by savoring each bite and focusing on flavors and sensations.

• Practice mindful walking by taking slow, deliberate steps and focusing on each breath.

• Deep, deliberate breathing can help manage stress and everyday chores.

4. Guided Meditation and Mindfulness Apps

• Use Guided Sessions: Access guided mindfulness meditations via apps or online resources.

• Mindfulness applications: Discovering user-friendly applications with guided meditations for all experience levels.

5. Mindfulness for Stress Reduction.

• Mindfulness can help develop stress awareness and identify triggers.

• Coping Strategies: Practice mindfulness to respond calmly to challenges, rather than responding impulsively.

6. Joining Mindfulness Communities:

• Participate in local or online mindfulness groups for support and shared experiences.

• Consider attending mindfulness retreats to deepen practice and develop community.

Practicing mindfulness meditation allows women to develop a greater awareness of their thoughts and emotions, resulting in a more balanced and serene attitude to life. Mindfulness meditation, as a potent stress-reduction strategy, may become a regular habit, improving general well-being.

Deep Breathing Exercises.

Deep breathing exercises are easy yet effective ways to reduce stress and promote relaxation. In this part, we look at a variety of deep breathing exercises designed specifically for women over 50, providing accessible techniques for managing anxiety and improving general well-being.

1. Diaphragmatic Breathing (Belly Breathing): Sit or lay comfortably.

• Position one hand on the chest and the other on the abdomen.

• Deeply inhale through the nose, letting the abdomen expand.

• Slowly exhale through pursed lips and feel the abdomen constrict.

2. The 4-7-8 Breathing Technique

• Laydown or sit in a relaxed position.

• Breathe in/Inhale quietly through your nose for a count of four.

• Hold your breath for a count of seven.

• Exhale thoroughly through your mouth for a count of eight.

• Repeat for many cycles.

3. Alternate Nostril Breathing (Nadi Shodhana): • Sit comfortably with a straight back.

• Close the right nostril with the right thumb and breathe in through the left.

• Close one nostril with the right ring finger, then exhale.

• Inhale via the right nostril, then shut it and exhale through the left.

• Repeat this process for a few breath cycles.

4. Box Breathing (Square Breathing): Inhale for a count of four.

• Hold your breath for a few seconds or count of four.

• Exhale for a count of 4.

• Hold your breath out for a count of 4.

• Repeat this cycle.

5. Sighing Breath: Inhale deeply through the nose.

• Sigh and exhale audibly.

• Repeatedly release tension.

6. Morning Breath Ritual

• Begin your day with mindful deep breathing.

• Inhale deeply and picture pleasant energy.

• Slowly exhale to release tension and negativity.

Incorporating deep breathing techniques into everyday routines helps women manage stress, relax, and improve their overall mental health. These exercises are adaptable to a variety of places and situations, making them effective tools for maintaining emotional equilibrium.

4. BUILDING A SUPPORT SYSTEMs
Nurturing Relationships

Meaningful ties with friends and family are critical for emotional well-being, particularly among women over the age of 50. This section highlights the value of fostering relationships and provides ways for developing strong, supportive ties.

1. Open communication.

• Express feelings honestly with loved ones.

• Active Listening: Demonstrate attentive and compassionate listening to enhance comprehension.

2. Quality Time • Prioritize Togetherness: Schedule time for shared experiences.

• Foster meaningful conversations to strengthen ties.

3. Setting Boundaries.

• Maintain balance via clear communication of personal limits.

• Respect others' boundaries and promote open communication.

4. Resolving Conflicts Constructively

• Effective Communication: Focus on understanding and resolving problems.

• Collaborate to discover mutually agreed solutions.

5. Celebrate Milestones and Achievements.

• Celebrate individual and team successes.

• Express gratitude: Show appreciation for each other's contributions and support.

6. Assistance During Challenges

• Empathy: Provide emotional support during difficult times.

• Team up to solve problems and overcome challenges.

7. Connecting with Like-Minded Communities

• Joining Social Groups: Join organizations, classes, or groups that correspond with your interests.

• Connect with like-minded folks through online communities.

8. Reconnecting with Distanced Relationships.

• Connect with friends and family who are not in frequent contact.
• Foster genuine ties via shared memories and experiences.

9. Developing Friendships

• Prioritize meaningful friendships over quantity.

• Invest time in maintaining and strengthening these friendships.

Nurturing connections creates a strong support system, providing emotional nourishment and a sense of belonging. By actively participating in the well-being of these relationships, women may face life's problems with confidence, knowing they have a network of supportive people by their side.

Seeking Professional Guidance.

In certain instances, getting professional help is an important and powerful step toward properly managing anxiety and stress. This section discusses the significance of professional support and explains ways for women over 50 to seek help when necessary.

1. Recognize the need for professional help.

• Recognize and address persistent stress or anxiety symptoms.

• Assess the impact of these problems on everyday life and well-being.

2. Professional Support Options • Therapy and Counseling: Individual or group therapy can help address underlying concerns.

• Consult a psychiatrist for a full examination and medication choices if necessary.

• Join support groups for specific difficulties and build a feeling of community.

3. Find a Qualified Professional

• Research and Recommendations: Get recommendations from reputable sources and look for experienced specialists.

• Verify the credentials and specialties of the selected mental health practitioner.

4. Setting up the first appointment

• Confidentiality: Initial consultations are non-judgmental.

• Encourage open communication by sharing issues and goals to foster collaboration.

5. Developing a Supportive Therapeutic Relationship

• Prioritize trust and comfort with the chosen professional.

• Regular attendance is essential for effective treatment interventions.

6. Involving Family and Loved Ones

• Include family members in treatment sessions to address collective dynamics.

• Educating help System: Educate loved ones on the value of professional help.

7. Using Employee Assistance Programs

• Consult EAPs for confidential counseling and mental health options.

• Professional Development Opportunities: Support mental health programs in the workplace.

8. Online Mental Health Resources.

• Use internet treatment platforms for distant counseling sessions.

• Educational Platforms: Discover online resources for information and coping skills.

Seeking professional help is a proactive and empowered option that shows a dedication to mental health and well-being. Women over the age of 50 can negotiate problems, acquire useful insights, and build effective coping techniques by consulting with mental health specialists.

5. HORMONAL HEALTH AND MENTAL WELLBEING

Understanding Hormone Changes

Hormonal changes have a substantial impact on women's emotional well-being, especially for those over the age of 50 who may be going through menopause. This section dives into the effects of hormone fluctuations and provides tips for managing mental wellness during this time.

1. Menopause, Hormonal Fluctuations

 Recognizing menopausal symptoms. Understand typical symptoms including hot flashes, nocturnal sweats, and mood changes.

• Recognize hormonal changes that cause emotional changes, such as fluctuations in estrogen and progesterone levels.

2. Emotional Effects of Hormonal Changes

• Address mood swings caused by hormone fluctuations.

• Hormonal changes might cause increased emotional sensitivity.

3. Physical Symptoms and Emotional Wellness

• Recognize the influence of physical complaints, such as sleeplessness or joint pain, on emotional well-being.

• Use comprehensive approaches to address physical and emotional issues.

4. Communication with Healthcare Providers.

• Schedule frequent check-ups to evaluate hormone levels and general wellness.

• Open Dialogue: Discuss emotional changes with healthcare practitioners and seek support.

5. Healthy Lifestyle Options for Hormone Balance

• Prioritize a balanced diet with foods that promote hormonal equilibrium.

• Regular exercise improves general well-being, including hormonal health.

6. Supplements and Hormone Replacement Therapy (HRT): Consult with Healthcare Providers. Discuss the possible advantages and hazards of taking supplements or using hormone replacement therapy.

• Make educated selections when adding these alternatives into your wellness strategy.

7. Mind-Body Practices to Increase Emotional Resilience

• Practice mindfulness meditation to reduce stress and build emotional resilience.

• Practice yoga and relaxation techniques to reduce emotional stress.

8. Community Support and Shared Experiences.

• Join Menopause Support Groups: Connect with other women going through similar hormonal changes.

• Share experiences and thoughts with others facing similar issues.

Understanding the complexities of hormone shifts is critical for navigating the emotional terrain throughout menopause. Women who embrace holistic techniques, seek expert assistance, and connect with supportive networks may traverse this time with fortitude and prioritize their emotional well-being.

Exploring Hormone Replacement Therapy (HRT)

Hormone Replacement Therapy (HRT) is a medical intervention that aims to relieve symptoms caused by hormonal changes, particularly during menopause. This section gives a summary of HRT, including possible advantages, drawbacks, and aspects to consider while researching this option.

1. Understanding Hormone Replacement Therapy.

• Introduction to HRT: Learn about its benefits and how it may correct hormonal abnormalities.

• Learn about the many hormones used in HRT, including estrogen and progesterone.

2. Potential benefits of HRT

• Relieve Menopausal Symptoms: Learn how hormone replacement therapy can help with hot flashes, nocturnal sweats, and mood swings.

• Bone Health: Learn how hormone replacement therapy (HRT) can improve bone density and reduce the risk of osteoporosis.

3. Considerations and Risks

• Emphasize personalized treatment strategies to meet unique needs.

• Assess personal health history with healthcare providers to identify possible risks and advantages.

4. Types of Hormone Replacement Therapy.

• Estrogen Therapy: Learn about the use of estrogen in hormone replacement therapy and its variants.

• Consider combining estrogen and progesterone in hormone replacement therapy for certain health needs.

5. Administrative Methods

• Learn about typical pill types of hormone replacement therapy (HRT).

• Consider using transdermal patches or gels for convenience and preference.

6. Monitoring and adjusting treatment.

• Regular health check-ups are crucial for monitoring the efficacy of HRT. • Adjustments can be made to the treatment plan depending on individual reactions and changing health needs, in collaboration with healthcare specialists.

7. Informed Decision Making

• Be informed of potential hazards related with HRT, including breast cancer and blood clotting.

• Encourage open communication with healthcare practitioners to make educated decisions based on personal health objectives.

8. Alternative Strategies for Hormonal Health

• Explore lifestyle modifications, such as food and exercise that can improve hormonal balance.

• Consider alternative treatments and holistic techniques in addition or instead of HRT.

9. Consultation with healthcare providers.

• Conduct a comprehensive health evaluation with healthcare providers to establish the appropriateness of HRT.

• Encourage open and honest conversation with healthcare providers to discuss issues and desires.

Exploring Hormone Replacement Therapy necessitates a deliberate and educated approach. Women may make informed decisions about their hormonal health throughout the menopausal transition by taking into account their specific health demands, potential advantages, and alternative techniques. It is critical to work closely with healthcare specialists to ensure tailored assistance throughout the procedure.

6. ENGAGING IN HOBBIES AND ACTIVITIES

Exploring New Interests.

Engaging in new activities and hobbies may be an effective technique for women over 50 to decrease stress, improve well-being, and restore a sense of purpose. This section fosters the discovery of new interests and offers advice on how to incorporate these passions into daily life.

1. Identifying personal interests.

• Reflective Exploration: Consider your particular interests and passions.

• Embrace curiosity and openness to explore new hobbies.

2. Attempting a Variety of Activities

• Experiment with a variety of activities to see what resonates.

• Open-Mindedness: Embrace new experiences.

3. Physical and creative pursuits.

• Engage in physical activities such as hiking, dancing, or yoga to promote overall well-being.

• Enjoy creative activities like painting, writing, or playing an instrument.

4. Attending Clubs and Classes

• Participate in local groups or classes to connect with others who share your interests.

• Enroll in classes to learn new skills and expertise.

5. Accepting Technology and Online Communities.

• Discover online courses and seminars.

• Connect with virtual communities and apps tailored to individual interests.

6. Balancing Alone and Social Activities.

• Enjoy autonomous activities.

• Social Engagement: Engage in group activities to interact and exchange experiences.

7. Setting Realistic Goals.

• Set attainable objectives to stay motivated.

• Celebrating Milestones: Recognize progress and achievements along the road.

8. Prioritizing Enjoyment Over Perfection • Embracing Imperfection: Allow for inquiry without striving for perfection.

• Prioritize enjoyment and pleasure from the activity.

9. Schedule Time for Interests

• Designate time slots for new hobbies in the weekly program.

• Establish a schedule for regular involvement in preferred activities.

10. Reflections on Personal Growth

• Periodic self-reflection on how new hobbies might enhance personal progress.

• Adapt to changing interests and preferences.

Exploring new interests is an exciting and rewarding approach for women over 50 to enrich their lives. Individuals who include a variety of activities into their daily routine might discover latent abilities, make new social connections, and infuse each day with energy and purpose.

7. COGNITIVE BEHAVIOURAL TECHNIQUES

Addressing Negative Thought Patterns

Negative thinking patterns can dramatically increase worry and tension. This section delves into ways for identifying and addressing negative thoughts, building a more optimistic and resilient attitude in women over 50.

1. Be Aware Of Negative Thoughts.

• Practice mindful observation to become aware of unpleasant ideas without judging them.

• Use journaling to identify negative thought patterns.

2. Challenge Negative Assumptions

• Reality Check: Challenge negative preconceptions.

• Seek evidence to support or refute negative ideas.

3. Use Positive Affirmations

• Use affirmative statements to counter negative self-talk.

• Incorporate affirmations in everyday activities for reinforcement.

4. Cognitive restructuring.

• Recognize typical cognitive distortions, including black-and-white thinking and catastrophizing.

• Reframe negative beliefs with a more balanced and realistic perspective.

5. Mindfulness Meditation: Thought Observation

• Use mindfulness meditation to notice ideas without judgment.

• Focus on your breath to eliminate cognitive chatter.

6. Gratitude Practices • Keep a daily gratitude journal to list things for which you are grateful.

• Practice Mindful Appreciation: Focus on positive parts of life, especially during hard times.

7. Seeking Professional Support • Therapeutic Intervention: Therapy can help resolve negative mental patterns.

• Collaborate with a mental health expert to create tailored coping strategies.

8. Developing Self-Compassion • Practice Kindness to Self: Treat yourself with the same compassion and understanding you show others.

• Embrace Imperfections: Recognize that perfection is impossible and errors are chances for progress.

9. Social Support For Positive Reinforcement.

• Surround yourself with positive people.

• Celebrate achievements with friends and family.

10. Mind-Body Practices to Maintain Emotional Balance

• Practice yoga and Tai Chi to calm and balance your mind and body.

• Deep breathing exercises can help relax the mind and disrupt negative thought processes.

Addressing negative thought patterns is a proactive way to manage anxiety and stress. By incorporating these tactics into their everyday lives, women over 50 may create a more positive outlook, fostering emotional resilience and improving overall well-being.

Setting Realistic Goals.

Setting realistic and achievable objectives is an essential component of good anxiety and stress management. This section advises women over the age of 50 on how to set achievable, meaningful objectives that add to a sense of success.

1. Clarifying priorities and values.

• Conduct reflective assessment to identify personal priorities and values.

• Ensure goals correspond with priorities.

2. Breaking Down Larger Goals.

• Divide major goals into smaller, more doable activities.

• Take a step-by-step approach to prevent feeling overwhelmed.

3. SMART Goal Setting.

• Specific: Clearly state the purpose and objectives.

• Establish measurable goals to measure progress and achievement.

• Ensure the aim is practical and doable.

• Align the aim with your beliefs and ambitions.

• Establish a timetable for reaching the goal.

4. Prioritizing Self-Care Goals

• Emphasize objectives for physical, mental, and emotional well-being.

• Prioritize self-care when balancing responsibilities.

5. Flexibility in Goal Adjustments.

• Recognize the need to adapting, accept to changing circumstances.

• Adapt to changing priorities and goals.

6. Set Incremental Milestones

• Set milestones to celebrate progress.

• Recognize little progress to boost motivation.

7. Managing Personal and Professional Goals

• Integrate personal and professional goals.

• Prioritize work-life balance by setting goals that lead to a satisfying existence.

8. Accountability and Support • Ensure accountability. Partners: Share your goals with a trustworthy friend or family member for mutual support.

• Seek professional counsel from a coach or mentor.

9. Increasing Confidence via Goal Achievement.

• Use achieved goals as positive reinforcement.

• Build self-efficacy by successfully completing goals.

10. Developing a Growth Mindset.

• Embrace obstacles as chances for progress.

• Embrace setbacks as learning opportunities instead than failures.

11. Reflecting on Goal Alignment and Well-Being

• Regularly evaluate goals to ensure they promote overall well-being.

• Adjust goals if they no longer promote personal progress or satisfaction.

Setting realistic objectives is a dynamic process that requires ongoing assessment and revision. By combining these ideas into goal-setting activities,

8. TIME MANAGEMENT AND PRIORITIZATION

Effective Time Management Strategies

Efficient time management is critical for women over 50 who want to balance several duties while reducing stress. This section discusses efficient time management tactics for increasing productivity and establishing a balanced daily routine.

1. Prioritizing tasks

• Identify urgent vs. significant jobs.

• Use the Eisenhower Matrix to prioritize tasks by categorizing them into four quadrants depending on their urgency and importance.

2. Planning a daily schedule

• Allocate time periods for different jobs or activities.

• Integrate a daily regimen for consistency and organization.

• Allow additional time for unanticipated disruptions or delays.

• Establish realistic time estimates for jobs to prevent overcommitting.

4. Using Technology Tools.

• Use calendar apps to arrange appointments, deadlines, and reminders.

• Task Management applications: Find applications to create to-do lists and track task fulfillment.

5. Delegating Responsibilities

• Identify chores that may be assigned to others.

• Clearly clarify expectations when distributing duties.

6. Avoid Multitasking.

• Prioritize quality over quantity: Focus on one assignment at a time.

• Reduce cognitive strain by eliminating excessive multitasking.

7. Effective Decision Making

• Decide quickly on little chores to minimize unnecessary delays.

• Develop explicit decision-making criteria based on goals and values.

8. Take Regular Breaks For Renewed Focus.

• Use the Pomodoro Technique to focus more effectively by breaking work into periods with brief pauses.

• Encourage physical activity during breaks, such as brief walks or stretches.

9. Managing Email and Communication • Scheduled Email Checks: Set particular times for monitoring emails.

• Use succinct communication strategies to reduce superfluous back-and-forths.

10. Saying 'No' when necessary.

• Establishing boundaries and saying 'no' to unnecessary obligations when overwhelmed.

• Prioritize personal well-being by setting personal time restrictions.

11. Regular review and adjustment.

• Weekly Review: Evaluate past week's actions and change tactics for the future week.

• Adapt to changing situations by being flexible and adjusting time management tactics accordingly.

12. Mindful Time Management • Present Moment Focus: Concentrate on the current work without distractions.

• Practice mindful transitions to improve clarity between activities.

Implementing excellent time management skills allows women over 50 to increase productivity, reduce stress, and live a more balanced and satisfying life. Individuals who combine these tactics with flexibility and self-compassion can maximize their time and energy for personal and professional well-being.

Prioritizing Self-Care.

Prioritizing self-care is critical for the well-being of women over 50, as it provides a foundation for stress management and improved overall quality of life. This section investigates numerous self-care techniques and methods for incorporating them into everyday routines.

1. Understanding Your Self-Care Needs

• Reflective Self-Assessment: Identify personal self-care requirements through reflection.

• Take a holistic approach to self-care, taking into account physical, mental, and emotional health.

2. Creating a Self-Care Routine

• Create a daily regimen for self-care to ensure consistency.

• Personalize routines to meet individual tastes and requirements.

3. Physical Wellbeing

• Regular exercise improves strength, flexibility, and cardiovascular health.

• Prioritize a well-balanced diet with adequate nutrition and hydration.

4. Mental and Emotional Health.

• Use mindfulness meditation or deep breathing techniques to manage stress.

• Engage in enjoyable hobbies, such as reading or listening to music, for therapeutic benefits.

5. Adequate Sleep • Establish a consistent sleep schedule for quality and enough rest.

• Create a pleasant and suitable sleep environment.

6. Connecting with Nature • Outdoor Activities: Engage in nature-related activities such as walking, gardening, or picnics.

• Natural sunshine can improve mood.

7. Social Connection • Prioritize emotional support by spending quality time with loved ones.

• Actively participate in social activities, groups, or classes to build connections.

8. Creativity and Hobbies.

• Engage in creative activities that provide joy and contentment.

• Stimulate your mind by learning new skills and hobbies.

9. Setting Limits and Saying 'No' • Establish clear limits to safeguard personal time and well-being.

• Practice assertive communication, including expressing 'no' without feeling guilty.

10. Professional Support • Seek therapy or counseling for emotional well-being and personal growth.

• Prioritize frequent health check-ups for both physical and mental health issues.

11. Digital Detox: • Take scheduled breaks from electronic gadgets to limit screen time.

• Encourage relaxation by setting aside weekends for unplugged activities.

12. Gratitude Practice • Reflect regularly on good elements of life to cultivate gratitude.

• Keep a gratitude diary to record moments of thankfulness.

13. Delegating Responsibilities • To prevent feeling overwhelmed, delegate work to others.

• Effective Communication: Communicate needs and expectations while delegating.

14. Self-Reflection: • Regularly review overall well-being and alter self-care activities as needed.

• Adaptability: Be open to adjust self-care practices to changing conditions.

Prioritizing self-care is a proactive and powerful way to manage stress and improve overall health. By incorporating these techniques into their everyday lives, women over 50 can build resilience, improve their feeling of well-being, and negotiate life's problems more easily.

9. MANAGING FINANCIAL CHALLENGES.

Effective financial management is critical for women over 50 in order to protect their financial well-being and decrease stress. This section delves into ways for overcoming financial issues and establishing a solid financial foundation.

1. Assessing the Financial Situation

• Evaluate your budget by reviewing income, spending, and savings.

• Assess existing debts, interest rates, and repayment choices.

2. Creating a Realistic Budget: • Prioritize basic costs such as housing, utilities, and groceries.

• Create or refill an emergency fund to handle unexpected expenditures.

3. Reduce Non-Essential Spending

• Reduce discretionary spending by identifying non-essential sectors.

• Negotiate cheaper service fees and investigate discounts.

4. Investigating Additional Income Sources.

• Consider side hustles like part-time or freelance employment to enhance your income.

• Monetize hobbies or talents.

5. Debt-Management Strategies

• Create a debt repayment strategy that prioritizes high-interest loans.

• Negotiate with creditors to explore repayment options.

6. Financial Education and Consultation.

• Access financial literacy materials to improve money management abilities.

• Consult financial advisors for specialized help.

7. Long-Term Financial Planning • Maximize retirement savings programs.

• Research low-risk investing options. 8. Review insurance policies for appropriateness and cost-effectiveness.

• Ensure proper health and life insurance coverage.

9. Legal and Professional Assistance.

• Seek legal counsel on financial problems including estate planning and debt relief.

• Optimize tax methods with the assistance of tax specialists.

10. Community Resources and Support.

• Explore government financial aid programs.

• Reach out to local community groups for financial support and resources.

11. Stress-Management Strategies

• Utilize mindfulness and relaxation strategies to reduce stress.

• Regular physical activity promotes mental and emotional well-being.

12. Create a Support System

• Encourage open communication with family members about financial issues and include them in solutions.

• Seek advice and support from people who have had similar financial challenges.

13. Celebrating Financial Milestones.

• Recognize accomplishments and improvements, no matter how minor.

• Create a reward system for meeting financial milestones.

14. Regular Financial Check-Ups

• Regularly examine financial objectives and alter methods as needed.

• Adaptable Plans: Be willing to adjust financial plans depending on changing circumstances.

Effective financial management requires a mix of strategic planning, continual education, and efficient use of available resources. Women over 50 can use these tactics to negotiate financial issues, build resilience, and move toward long-term financial security.

Seeking Financial Guidance.

Seeking financial advice is a proactive step for women over 50 in navigating complicated financial environments, making educated decisions, and securing their financial well-being. This section delves into ways for receiving and implementing financial advice.

1. Clarifying Financial Goals

• Defining objectives: Clearly define your short- and long-term financial goals.

• Prioritize goals based on present needs and future aspirations.

2. Professional Financial Advisors

• CFP (Certified Financial Planners): Consult with authorized specialists for complete financial planning.

• Consult accountants for tax planning and financial strategies.

3. Financial Education • Self-Education: Read reliable financial books and use internet tools to educate yourself.

• Attend financial seminars or courses to improve financial literacy.

4. Government and Nonprofit Resources

• Explore government resources for financial guidance and help.

• Connect with non-profit groups offering financial counseling services.

5. Online Financial Tools.

• Use budgeting applications to track costs and manage funds.

• Use online investing platforms for convenient financial planning.

6. Peer Networks And Support Groups.

• Participate in financial networking events to meet with colleagues and share ideas.

• Join financial support groups to receive guidance and encouragement.

7. Legal Consultation • Consult with estate planning attorneys for advice on wills, trusts, and estate administration.

• Seek legal help for complex financial issues like bankruptcy or debt restructuring.

8. Banks and Financial Institutions

• Banks offer financial consulting services.

• Consult credit counseling agencies for debt management help.

9. Retirement Plan Consultants

• Seek advice from retirement planning experts.

• Consult Social Security Advisors for guidance on optimizing retirement benefits.

10. Educational Courses and Webinars

• Enroll in financial literacy classes provided by educational institutions.

• Get professional views on financial subjects through online seminars and podcasts.

11. Family Discussions and Sharing Wisdom

• Hold open communication with family members about financial objectives and obstacles.

• Encourage intergenerational learning by sharing financial knowledge and experiences with younger family members.

12. Regular Financial Check-Ups

• Conduct yearly financial reviews with advisors to evaluate objectives and strategy.

• Monitor investment portfolios and make adjustments as appropriate.

13. Insurance Professionals

• Consult with insurance specialists to guarantee appropriate coverage.

• Assess financial risks with insurance specialists to handle them effectively.

14. Chartered Financial Analysts (CFA)

• Consult CFAs for detailed investment analysis and recommendations.

• Seek help for developing and maintaining investment portfolios.

Seeking financial advice entails a combination of professional knowledge, continuous education, and utilizing accessible resources. Women over the age of 50 may make solid financial decisions, maximize their resources, and strive toward a financially stable future by taking a multifaceted approach and keeping informed.

10. ONLINE COMMUNITIES FOR PEER SUPPORT

Online groups give great opportunities for women over 50 to interact with others, exchange experiences, and provide mutual support. This section discusses the advantages of joining online communities and recommends places where women may discover supportive networks.

1. Advantages of Online Communities.

• Connect with others experiencing similar life stages and problems.

• Access help from home, removing geographical constraints.

•Diverse perspectives: Learn from people from different backgrounds.

2. Social Media Groups.

• Discover Facebook groups focused on women's health, wellness, and lifestyle.

• Join professional groups on LinkedIn to network and discuss career-related topics.

3. Forum and Discussion Boards

• Participate in appropriate subreddits spanning diverse interests and experiences.

• Join health and wellness forums to discuss physical and emotional well-being.

4. Wellness and Lifestyle Platforms.

• Find online wellness communities that promote holistic well-being, exercise, and healthy living.

• Follow lifestyle sites with active comment sections for community engagement.

5. Learning Platforms.

• Join forums for online courses to exchange learning experiences.

• Participate in educational platforms such as webinars and virtual events to promote peer learning.

6. Support Groups for Specific Challenges.

• Find online support groups for specific health issues.

• Connect with financial support groups to discuss difficulties and solutions.

7. Local Community Websites

• Join city or region-specific online communities to stay up to date on local events and debates.

• Use neighborhood-specific applications to connect and support your community.

8. Book clubs and Literary Communities

• Participate in online book groups based on your reading choices.

• Join literary forums to stimulate intellectual interactions.

9. Parenting and Grand parenting Communities.

• Connect with other parents and grandparents through online parenting forums.

• Join groups dedicated to the experiences of grand parenting.

10. Professional Networking Platforms.

• Join industry-specific groups to expand your professional network.

• Join LinkedIn Groups for professional discussions and networking possibilities.

11. Hobbies and Interests.

• Hobby-Based Platforms: Join groups based on common hobbies or interests.

• Join crafting and DIY Forums to connect with others who enjoy crafting or DIY projects.

12. Mental Health and Wellness Communities

• Join online communities that promote mental health and well-being.

• Discover mindfulness applications with community features to reduce stress.

13. Fitness and Wellness Apps.

• Participate in fitness challenges on applications that promote community connection.

• Connect with peers on sites for holistic health tracking.

14. Senior-Specific Communities

• Senior Social Networks: Discover platforms built for seniors to connect and share experiences.

• Join Retirement Forums to discuss retirement and post-retirement life.

Online groups offer a safe space for women over 50 to interact, exchange advice, and find fellowship. Individuals that actively participate in these communities have access to a variety of knowledge, make connections, and feel a feeling of belonging in a digital realm.

Encouragement of Ongoing Self-Care

Prioritizing self-care is a continuous process that greatly improves the well-being of women over 50. This section provides encouragement and practical advice for maintaining a commitment to continual self-care.

1. Celebrating Small Victories.

• Celebrate progress towards self-care objectives, no matter how minor.

• Recognize and praise yourself for successes.

2. Responding to Changing Needs

• Be flexible in adapting self-care practices based on changing circumstances and needs.

• Adapt your self-care habits based on your body and emotions.

3. Mindful Living • Prioritize present moment awareness in self-care routines.

• Practice thankfulness by focusing on the good parts of your life.

4. Diversifying Self-Care Practices: • Continuously investigate and incorporate new self-care activities.

• Take a holistic approach to self-care, balancing physical, mental, and emotional needs for overall wellness.

5. Prioritizing 'Me Time' • agenda regular self-care time into your weekly agenda.

• Enjoy guilt-free self-care by prioritizing your well-being.

6. Reflecting on Benefits

• Keep a notebook to track the beneficial impact of self-care practices. • Reflect on how self-care improves your overall quality of life.

6. Incorporating Joyful Elements

• Incorporate joyful activities into your self-care regimen.

• Rediscover your childlike wonder and curiosity.

7. Accepting Imperfection

• Recognize that self-care is about nourishing oneself rather than striving for perfection.

• Take setbacks as chances to learn on how to and improve.

8. Connecting with Nature • Explore the outdoors and experience nature's healing power.

• Take attentive nature walks, focusing on the sights, sounds, and feelings around you.

9. Continuous Self-Education

• Adopt a lifelong learning mentality to discover new self-care habits.

• Stay educated on holistic well-being by reading, articles, and attending seminars.

10. Positive Affirmations: • Integrate positive affirmations into your everyday routine.

• Repeat phrases that promote self-love and acceptance.

• Schedule frequent check-ins with healthcare experts for a comprehensive health examination.

11. Be Kind to Yourself

• Self-Kindness: Treat yourself with the same compassion and understanding you show others.

• Promote self-love via rituals like self-massage or self-care.

Remember that continuing self-care is a journey, not a destination. By tackling it with patience, adaptation, and a dedication to your well-being, you may empower yourself to live a full and balanced life. Each moment of self-care is an investment in your health and happiness.